zendoodle coloring

Bright Side

zendoodle coloring

Bright Side

Words of Optimism to Color and Display

illustrations by
Bonnie Lynn Demanche

CASTLE POINT BOOKS

NEW YORK

www.castlepointbooks.com

The Castle Point Books trademark is owned by Castle Point Publishing, LLC.
Castle Point books are published and distributed by St. Martin's Publishing Group.

ISBN 978-1-250-27975-0 (trade paperback)

Our books may be purchased in bulk for promotional, educational, or business use.
Please contact your local bookseller or the Macmillan Corporate and Premium
Sales Department at 1-800-221-7945, extension 5442, or by email
at MacmillanSpecialMarkets@macmillan.com.

First Edition: 2022

10 9 8 7 6 5 4 3 2 1

Hope is simply the dreams of those who are awake

Very little in life is as Beautiful as spring's first Blooms

THE DARKEST HOURS YIELD TO DAWN'S GLORIOUS LIGHT